# LIFE IN WORDS

## R WOOD

Rick Wood Publishing

# About the Author

Rick Wood is a British writer born in Cheltenham.

His love for writing came at an early age, as did his battle with mental health. After defeating his demons, he grew up and became a stand-up comedian, then a drama and English teacher, before giving it all up to become a full-time author.

He now lives in Loughborough, where he makes his living from writing horror - and, more recently, poetry.

# Those Perfect Flaws

I want to be your stretch marks.

I want to be that mole by your mouth that you had
    surgically removed.

I want to be those perfect flaws you hate
Yet those things you hate are the thing
I love.

I'm sorry this couldn't work.
I'm sorry I couldn't be that wrinkle on your forehead,
That premature sign of ageing,
That thing you see but no one else can.

I want to be that hit song that was stuck in your head
So you deleted it off your iPhone with
The words going round and round
And round
And round.

I want to be your closed fist.
I want to latch onto your soul that does not exist
In your belief as you're an atheist,
I want to be that god you vilify
But don't hate
Just know does not exist.

I want that blemish, be that scar,
Be the drugs in your chemist you used to depart
Your mind from its illness.

I want to be those stretch marks.

I want to be that illness
And be that cure

But I don't think that's what you want.

At least not anymore.

# Flickers

When I think back,
Rarely, but sometimes,
As I clean or make a curry
Or wash up or cook or study
Or whatever mundane chore brought you into my mind,
I don't think I think of happiness.

But I don't think of sadness either.

Regret has no place in my thoughts,
Refusal of recollection or
Refusal to even mention isn't
Down to an error
Or mistake
But a lack of need
To open the treasure chest
And find there's
Still nothing there.

Controlling, yes

You were,
And I'm not sure you even know that,
At least not commonly
Knowingly or consciously.

It's not that I hate you
Or like you
It's just that I
Don't love you.

Is that okay?

It's been years, after all.

And if I was out walking
Shopping or with my phone out talking
And I saw you
In your place
And I did a double take
I'd say how are you
Hello
But I know
You would just keep marching
Covering your face and arching
Your back with pride
And keeping it all inside.

That hurts.

That if we were meeting
There'd be no greeting
And it's not me feeling
Anything for you but
Disappointment

That we can't be like old friends
Instead of like this
As an arch nemesis.

Do I regret?
No, but I bet
If I was to ask you
You'd say yes,
Actually,
I do.

# How Did You Know

My father sold my childhood for the lowest bid,
A bid funded by cigarettes and booze,
Then he'd wake in the morning set to be a good dad,
Lift his arm, drop it, and hit snooze.
For someone who lived his life on benefits
You never saw the benefits of time,
And that life you thought you were crushing all night,
It was never yours, it was mine.

I booked lots of appointments for parents evening,
Rushed from teacher to teacher til we were done,
Do you remember all those wonderful comments?
No, you didn't, because you didn't come.
I started a fight with a girl who was happier than me
And I was suspended for five days,
When you came home I told you what I had done;
You laughed, and you gave me praise.

When I cried I was loud enough to be heard from
    downstairs

But you'd already passed out at the pub,
Through the door you burst with your fists in the air
and I waited til they turned to a hug.
You cried and you told me how I was worthless and ugly,
That my brain worked a little slow.
You're right, I guess, I'm worthless and stupid –
But you don't know me, so how did you know?

# Pray For Me

Don't pray for me
  For prayer is the excuse of indulgence
  Screams behind closed fists
  Are but silent indulgences unanswered
  PRAY FOR THE VICTIMS
  An online status
  Replaces
  Donations deserving of place in spaces of haters
  Religion helps the world does
  it?
  When prayers pay the price of help and you feel
  Vilified
  Lavish luxuries laid out behind the keys of a message board
  Guilt unburdened by three meaningless words
  Do more or do nothing
  God is not real nor is he an excuse

# A Momentary Flicker

Day one.
Or was it day zero?
We met on ground one, or ground zero
- again, can't remember –
And I thought you were the
Answer the
Solution but
You were barely the question –
You were the cause.

Innocent enough,
Scorned by your past
And willing to change fast,
When there's a will there's a way but for you
A way out.

Slathered in green and
Unashamedly jealous.
I succumbed and pampered,
Lied and enacted

The words it took to quell your worries
Temporarily.
Always temporarily.

And I wonder if
Nowadays
When you're vacuuming
Cooking
Walking
Looking or talking
Whether you stop,
Think of me.
Briefly.
Then walk and move on.

These words are that thought.

Replacing what ifs with it's done.

# Ants

I killed ants as a child.
I killed ants and I
Stomped on them.
Stomped around
Like it was a game and
I was a
Giant.

Nobody told me murder was wrong
When it came to ants.

So why are you so surprised
When someone stomps on you?

# Skills

Every word restarts an unexpected fuse,
Expected but for the words that quelled it.
A wayward stranger's glance can make me
Ruin
My girlfriend's weekend.
Don't call me fire I am ice,
Until I'm sharpened to a point and look at what I've
      done.
You request information
Explanation
That a childhood can't excuse.
Stand beside me and I'll open the door.
But stand in front of me and stop
In a supermarket or a café or shop or the street
And it will take the restraint of an unwaged war
To not break you
Red face you
Encase you
In wrath you deserve but never foresaw.

Save me or forgive me.

But never accept me.

Or do, though I'll never
Regret anything as much as regret.

# Graveyards

The graveyard looks nice in the summer.
Stone rock clear,
Marked lettering visible,
The flowers restocked.

It's only the winter
When it's not convenient
To remember
The dead.

# How You Miss Me

I'm going back to sleep.

The only place where I care
To see you at night
So I can just
Wake up again.

Fumbling for your silhouette
In my curtain enclosed cell
And push what isn't there
From my thoughts.

I'm really starting to think
You don't actually exist
And you just haunt me
With your persistence
Insistence
For instance
Your tirade of abuse
From my subconscious

To my nightmares.

But I see you.

Same as you were in my mind.

Dripping with aggression
And cruellest intention
To concede my life as misery
For as long as you
Still love me.

Hate is a funny way of
Showing your affection.

You're not even worth a mention.

# Message Read

Old acquaintance
I used to know
Back in the days
When we knew that making mistakes
Was something
Exclusive
To youth...

Sometimes I look you up
On Facebook
To see how you've done
And I'm sad to see
You've all kept in touch.

Tagged in each other's photos,
Hugs at your weddings,
Pictures with your kids,
And statuses
Where you have all gloated
About your meal.

Not that there's anything
Remotely bad
About keeping up
With your oldest friends
I just thought that
Maybe,
Possibly,
Hopefully –
*I'd be one of them.*

Maybe it's not that,
And I shouldn't resent you that much
For not keeping in touch
Or for the line going cold
As it could have been my fault
I mean,
I didn't email much,
Maybe only once;
So if I didn't keep up correspondence
How could I expect you to
Drop me a line when you're around
Or back in town
Or when you're feeling down
Like I'm someone
Worth thinking of.

Or maybe it is my fault.
I am a nomad
You hadn't the desire
To talk to
After school was dead.
Perhaps it's up to me
For being
So

Completely.
Indiscreetly,
Unobtrusively,
Unlikable.

Loud.
Boastful.
Showing off and
Hard to love,
Hard to want to keep in touch
With someone so arrogant,
So depressed,
So diagnosed,
And someone who struggled
So much with
Life
When we were too young
To really know
What life was.

I found out who my real friends could be
The day we left for university,
As only my real friends bothered to keep in touch
And now I surround myself
With those friends
And only those friends.

Unfortunately, I surrounded myself with
No one.

So either I never had any real friends,
They do not exist,
Or it's just that I'm not worth
A five-minute message.

I could email you.

But I did once.

And all I saw when I returned to my phone
Was one little line,
Two words
That summed up everything,
So completely,
So succinctly,
And said everything that needed to be said:

*Message read.*

# An Online Forum

You liberal feminazi
Constantly remonstrating at me
Like a died hair fatty
Who thinks they are right how can that be?

694EVA argues with ClamydiaBoyShit
About the ins and out of Brexit
On twitter as it's the dacorum
To use this as the forum
To affect change and to implore them
To change the laws but you only bore them.

State an opinion with limited characters
Never thinking about external factors
Behind the keyboard with the laughters
And feeling smug in the afters
A response always so blunt
To an educated opinion you've researched and learnt
To have anonymous trolls on the hunt
Tell you to fuck off you fucking cunt.

Elegantly put, of course,
An opinion answered by an opinion
The blank-faced profile picture allows
But if we met in person
In a café or a park
At midday or after dark
Would you be so bold
Or would you shrink down and fold.

I hate you tory bastards –
Go fuck your mum liberal scum –
Words made to affect a change
That affect nothing but a young person
Merely expressing a thought
On social media or a message board
Who was somehow unduly caught
By the undergrowth of society who ought

To go on a march
A demonstration
Instead of this senile
Act of masturbation
Where abuse is the answer
To your frustration
Never quite sure
Who you're hating.

Grow up or go home.
And let all the liberal feminazis free
While you stay in your prison cell and beam
over your computer screen.

# Burden

I am a million things in one
But I am not the man they make movies about.
Always the lover, sometimes the friend,
Never both but with you.

Is it what you wanted, an ill-famed nuisance?

Supporting the oddball on the screen is admirable;
It's a character we admire in the way
We wish to be admired.

Reality
Is the moment you wake up
And find it's after the happy ever after.

Hollywood wrapped fairy tales into a package
Bow-tied it
Hand-signed it
Dear you, have this lie,
Keep it on the pedestal

All relationships can climb to and stumble
On a sycophantic rock.
Make the face of the package
Clean
Spotless in a way that no one is ever spotless.

Teenagers ridden in acne
Watch
The smooth-faced made-up bastard
In a teenage soap opera.

I'm a mess.
Difficult.
Unbearable even to my own misguided
Misled
Self-image
That it's okay to be who I am.

That's what they teach us, isn't it?

That if they hate us, it's their problem?

So where are those that don't hate?

Those friends
Who knew me
Well enough
Not to stick around

Tightly formed in years
And broken in a
Moment of truth.

Who needs them?

A sixty-five-inch plasma showed me
A sixty-five-inch story of
A sixty-five-inch man to
Whom no one thought was too small.

Love me or hate me.

Except, it's not that simple, is it?

Because you always choose the latter.

# Interlude

What if a one syllable word
Had the chance to change the world.

Wouldn't that be great?

# Cocoon

People clamber round the gates
Lolling and JKing with their mates
Arranging nightly sought-after dates
and I'm comparing myself to everyone else around me

Made up on the face like a thick icing cake
Spreading no love but texting their hate
Ego's always on time but they're always late
and I'm comparing myself to everyone else around me

Laugh in the smile of hostile authority
Whisper to your friends about this monstrosity
Eating your pills 20mg for tea
and I'm comparing myself again

But a flamenco am I, with one leg to stand on
Blood shot eye, with no where to land on
But flying in the sky, reach out put my hand on
And I'm being compared to vulgar minds around me

# Fool

This is an ode to the ineptitude
Who hate those of us who are just being rude,
You have the trigger and you're far too into it,
And quite obviously too illiterate,
An orange face hiding a thug
Coming across as that guy in the pub
That preaches prejudice with misery
And you sit safe in the knowledge he's not taken
    seriously.

How did this happen?
They gave common sense a rest.
From the high of Obama
And what looked like progress

To this.
And now we're living it.
Nuclear weapons at his disposal;
It's scary isn't it?

Optimism abound with a treaty's pledge
Now the world is poised unbalanced on the edge
Ready to tumble eventually
And plunge us all into world war three,

A flag full of stars
Before a face full of hate,
On your knees with no salute
Hoping it's not too late,
You wreck your country
Then take the mick
By labelling this protest
As unpatriotic;

That's ironic

Once you've changed what that flag meant
How can you salute what it now represents,
Because you did this without the consent
Of the educated public whose patience is spent,

And now you make claims so wild
Then react when someone complains
Throw your hands into the air like a child
While we just hope that these things will change.

# The Fight

Eight sides.
Bare chest.
A gracious loser
Shakes hands with
The winner with
A battered face.

There are rules but they are pointless.
There are spectators who pay too much
To watch two figures
In the distance
Batter through years of training.

It's time, he says.
We've all been waiting for
The sponsors to be read out,
Making it blatant how much
Money rules
The gladiators.

Two entrants. Four fists.
A corner that is a side.
I can see muscle,
Tattoos on chests,
This team talk is sponsored by
Bloody noses and
Mangled faces.

There can only be one winner:
The man who makes the profit
And has never fought a fight in their life.

# Four Letters

Four letters excuse all sins,
Make excuses for lies we're living in,
Never considering or contemplating
Asking or debating
What those four letters mean.

It's closer to hate than it is to like,
The separation between both of us when we fight,
They share no letters but they share a cause,
An unwilling participant out of force,
Turning four letters to hate and heavy to light.

I'm sorry, I *blank* you,
The blank implies your apology is true
But no lessons can come out of your verse
That was quieter than actions and as quiet as words.

Do it then.
I dare you.

Do it or don't
Because I can't bare you
Using that word as your excuse.
Again and again like it's not something you choose,
Let's cut the letters as I cut you loose.

Four letters ignited my fuse.

# No Choice

It was never death that tempted me.
It was the absence of life.
No choice
Or
Not one I could
Find.

You're only as good as the friends you keep
But I keep
No one.
Nothing.

I learnt to talk
Before I learnt to
Pay for my
Words.
Just like I learnt to die
Before I learnt to
Live.

I wrote a poem about sleep.
Then I woke up.

I'm grateful for failing.

For an attempt
That hid
Like an eclipse
That refused to give way.

Before she came along I
Thought relationships were
The prison cells
Rather than
The first step outside
And the first breath of freedom.

Grateful
For the error,
Not in judgement
But in my forever.

Never
Again will I wish
For an easy choice.

I'm fixed
But a service is still required.

# Small

When I stand next to you
Two foot taller
I feel
Funsize
Child height
Inadequate light for me to grow

Talk to me like I talk to
Petulance
A pram surrounded by toys
And a toddler angelic

You take my light

You stunt my growth

You make me feel my age
Divided by ten
And fixed in place
My roots in the ground

And branches empty.

I say something I'm scalded
I can't speak my mind
As I'm grounded.

Leave me alone.

Stay, but stand back.

I can't take another instruction.

# Losing You

Losing you at all would be insufferable. Losing you to
hate would kill me.

Hate inhabits you like milk through hot water, acid
through fire, an infestation through a happy child, a
constant itching,

Taking over your blood, sweating through your poors,
detest ruminating throughout you like poisoned
blood.

It is dead skin flaking off living cells, it is the flesh no
longer useful brushed away and discarded.

An acne scar. Remnants of a temporary blemish of the
flesh, gone in days, but visible for years.

A cognitive dissonance. An intellectual failure delaying
the basis of functioning.

Psychodynamic development dulled into destitute
ideology;

It's socialisation, but failed, an imitation of a fake form
of flattery parents weren't afforded.

Forgiveness. Our words we use to make up. Meeting

minutes made with sentiment and good will sent out
    but never opened.
The Oedipus complex, complexity confounding
    creativity into a succinct set of sexual stalemates, so
    unrealistic.
Our free will fairly afforded formed into frail fractures of
    society forewarned.
Coffee ground into grinding teeth. Goliath to the game.
Either do something worth telling or tell something
    worth hearing. Don't tell me words. Don't tell me
    things you will go back on the next time our hate
    takes over.
Choose me. Choose forever. Choose to love me. Choose
    to work at it.
To choose me is to choose forgiveness.
We are not perfect.
I hate to think hate is all we have.

# Your God

Fictitious
And suspicious
And most of the time malicious
Spent time trying to fix us
But never seemed to lift us.

You require
A power higher
Like a drug and He's the supplier
Never knowing why you try to
Believe the outrageous liar.

You say just take a look
At this book
And you'll see that you mistook
That isn't down to luck
He's a superior being so he just took what he took.

But there's this thing that's just immense
And it's called common sense

It goes with evidence
Reasoning and sitting on the fence
Not believing nonsense at our expense.

So let's shut away the bile
We can all give it a trial
Step in my shoes and walk a mile
Take a walk you'll find worthwhile
So you can stop believing in the past and stop living in
    denial.

And once you stop being so infantile
That day our beliefs will reconcile.

# The Great Voyage

We're heading out today
With doggy treats and doggy bags,
We may not change the world
But we'll chase a few leaves and bark at a few cats,
It's nothing too profound
Just two lives and a lot of love,
We're going out today
We've got each other and that's enough.

We're going out today
We're off our leads and she's running at kids,
It may not seem too much
But it's another thing to tick off the list,

We're away from home
But I'm pretty sure that we're not missed,
We'll stop off for a coffee
And to think bout how it can't get better than this

# Don't Be

When the flames finished burning and my ashes have
    been sieved
When you think and think on how it came to this
When you take my stuff decide what's hers and
    what's his
Don't be sad for what isn't, be glad for what is.

When my body is scattered and you've said your
    goodbyes
And you try and decipher the truth from the lies
And you think that I spent my life hurting inside
Don't be sad for my lows, be glad for my highs.

There's reason for tears in such times I suppose
As pain makes way and anger's harnessed and grows
Desperate to feel me you take a sniff of my clothes
Just don't be sad that I fell, be glad that I rose.

All those times that we fought and we pushed and we
    shoved

We fell out and we cried then made up and we hugged
We shed tears for the times that we seemed to shed
    blood
Don't be sad that we hated, be glad that we loved.

All those times that we pushed and we pulled and we hit
We shoved and raged and lamented and kicked
Just look at what we were covering love with
So don't be sad that I'm dead, be glad that I lived.

# Afterword

After writing this short, succinct collection of poems about experiences in my life, I thought that you may lose something by not knowing the context to each and every word.

Then again, poetry isn't about definite explanations, is it? Some words can mean something to me when I put them on the page, but by the time they enter your mind, you can turn them to something different – hopefully as they resonate with your own life experiences, thoughts and values.

But I thought it would be amiss to publish this set of poems without giving some explanation as to what inspired the words I put in each carefully chosen lexical choice.

So this is a brief afterword to relay the experiences and thoughts behind the words you have just read and, hopefully, enjoyed.

I started the book with *Those Perfect Flaws* – which I actually wrote with far greater optimism than I think ended up going into the resulting poem. If you ignore the a few of the more downbeat lines, then you can see the poem as I intended it: about how those things your hate about yourself are most likely those things that someone loves. That stretch mark, that mole (which a girlfriend I had as a teenager intended to have removed) and those scars – those are the things that make you unique, and you should never wish to change.

*Flickers* was about how I had to become the subject of hatred for an ex-girlfriend to get over me. I get that it's easier to move on from someone you despise, but it makes me sad that, after so much, I have to be hated. And this doesn't come from any love that is left for this ex, as I make clear in the poem – this comes from a sadness that, having both moved on, if we bumped into each other by some form of coincidence, she would still cling onto that hate and refuse to say hello. After sharing part of your life with someone, I think that is really sad.

*How Did You Know* came from my four years working as a teacher. In my first two years I worked in one of the roughest schools in the country - which involved breaking up fights, being sworn at and removing weapons on a weekly basis - as well as being assaulted twice. There was one girl who was a nightmare to teach, but was such a great personality - and it broke my heart to be aware of the home she came from. She really wanted parents who cared - to the point that she booked parent's evening appointments and went to them on her own. She was only thirteen. It was tough to witness such a remarkable, albeit nightmarish, child, who had so much potential, but would never achieve that potential because of the background she came from.

The fourth poem was the first of a few poems in this book that begins to express my passionate atheist beliefs – but it wasn't intended as a piece of atheism, but rather a piece of action. When someone in the news is hurt, or a large disaster happens, the hashtag #prayfor(insertname) starts to trend, and people quote this on social media all the time. But, ultimately, it means nothing, does it? You could donate money, go on a protest, do something with your time – but to say 'pray for (whoever)' you get to show that you care without actually having to care. My attitude is either do something or don't bother – but don't pretend with these meaningless words. At no point has praying ever helped these people, but action has.

*A Momentary Flicker* is a kind of sequel to *Flickers*. It's about a moment, when you are just doing something you would normally do, whatever mundane activity it is – and suddenly someone from your past pops into your head. They stay there for a moment, then leave. This poem is that moment.

When I was a child, I don't know about you, but I used to stomp on ants as a game. No one would tell me not to – after all, I was only stomping on a few little creatures. In reality, I was murdering innocent animals that just happened to be smaller than me. Part of the reason I am an atheist is because I see us as the ants – if there is something greater, we aren't able to understand it, same as ants can't understand us. So if there is a god – why wouldn't it stomp on us?

From a child to an adult, I have struggled with my temper. I have had anger management both as a child, and as an adult. That is what *Skills* is about. I think "a wayward stranger's glance can make me ruin my girlfriend's weekend" is one of the most apt, well-articulated lines I've ever written – if a person giving me a dodgy look or says something to me I don't like, then that could blow my fuse; my girlfriend would be upset by outburst, and I would have ruined her weekend.

Safe to say, I'm doing a lot better in controlling such things now!

*Graveyards* was something I wrote when doodling. I think it is a metaphor, and is as much to your interpretation as it was to the wandering hand that wrote it.

*How You Miss Me* is along the lines of a few poems that reference love in this book. It's strange, really, as I didn't think of myself as such a cynic! But I think I regret - no, regret is too strong a word; I lament upon how relationships sometimes have to end. With anger and hatred. And this is about an ex who turned spiteful because they were 'still in love' - and had a strange way of showing it.

*Message Read,* however, is about a specific moment I had when looking at Facebook. I noticed some friends from school that I had lost contact with hadn't lost contact with each other – they were attending one of their weddings, making the effort to keep in touch. This made me wonder – what's wrong with me? Why not keep in touch with me? I had huge issues with mental health in my last year of school that they didn't cope with well, and I often wonder if that is why they weren't bothered about including me in their reunions.

Social media has many downsides, of course. *An Online Forum* speaks about the online abuse that comes out of a simple debate. If two people have different opinions online then such words as 'feminazis' are slung about like it actually has meaning. It's worrying how much anonymity allows your supposedly average person to be vile and abusive to a stranger. This poem had some quite harsh language in that I debated whether to include - but this is the language flung about online, and I decided to keep a close relationship to reality, despite the shocking nature of the words.

*Burden* is about how difficult I am to be in a relationship with. I have numerous mental health issues that I hate having to inflict on the one I love. It can't be easy – and it's unfair that movies make us think that a happily ever after means love will conquer such problems. In reality, what happens after that happily ever after?

At just three lines long, *Interlude* is the shortest poem in the book, which is consistent with the main subject of this poem - shortness within language. You'd have thought powerful ideas would have powerful words that extend over a great many syllables, yet so few do. Love, war, god - all words that inspire greatness and evil, yet are so succinct that you could use them in a sentence without it even being noticed.

Despite what issues I may have, I am not a person who often cares what others think. And it surprises me when other people seem to compare themselves to everyone else – people who have just as many issues as them – and that's what led to *Cocoon*.

*Fool,* my only piece of political poetry, is a commentary on one of the most dangerous, misogynistic, racist world leaders negatively influencing lives today. I hesitated to include a potentially divisive poem - but this is about my outlook on the world, and as it is my book, I decided that I shouldn't have to hide it.

*The Fight* brings a slight break from some of the heaviness of my words to reference one of my favourite things to watch on TV - the UFC. Which is strange, as it's just two people in an octagon cage battering each other in the hope of knocking them out. While I watch this, consciously aware of how primitive it is, I often think about how it isn't so different to gladiators in an arena of a few hundred years ago - except the risk of death of slightly less. Still, the fighters get paid a lot for the 'hard work' of the entertainment - which makes it odd that the ones who receive the most money from the fight, i.e. the promoters, the betters, the presidents - are the ones who have probably never been in a fight in their life.

Forgiveness is a strange thing – it seems as if 'love' means you should instantly forgive. Isn't that a cop out for when something has been done that's awful? *Four Letters* is about how love isn't about telling someone you love them, but showing your love by how you treat them and what you do.

*No Choice* makes references to my girlfriend I am happily settled with now. "Before she came along I thought relationships were the prison cells" states very clearly how I felt about relationships before I met her – I thought it was normal to feel trapped and as if there were lots of things I couldn't do. My girlfriend pushes me to do all of these things and to explore life. Which leads me onto *Losing You*.

My strongest piece of atheist poetry follows in *Your God,* where I chose not to hold back about what I really think about the belief in a superior being in the religious sense.

I ended the book with two of my most emotive poems.

*The Great Voyage* is about Rosie, my shorkie puppy. I love her to bits, as I hope this poem shows.

And *Don't Be* is my reaction to death. My hope is that, once I'm gone, I can remain a positive influence on those that knew me – rather than a feeling of sadness and despair. I recently lost a relative who wished that, and his wake was very much a celebration rather than misery.

At my funeral, I wish for everyone to show up in clown costumes. I just love the image of my dad reluctantly being coerced into a big red nose and face paint, feeling obliged as it was my dying wish.

Now that would be a great send off!

# Sign up for One Poem a Week

For your free poems visit
www.lifeinwordspoetry.com/sign-up

For more information about Life in
Words, visit the website


www.lifeinwordspoetry.com

Life in Words Volume 2: Mental Health
and Me is OUT NOW